Goddess GRATITUDE *Journal*

tu-anh love

ISBN: 979-8-9863822-0-3 (Paperback)
ISBN: 979-8-9863822-1-0 (Hardcover)

Book interior & cover design by Taylor Ahlstrom.
Printed by Amazon Publishing in the United States of America.
First printing edition 2022.

"Envision it, it will come to you.
Desire it, you shall have it.
Take ownership of it,
it will be yours."

-tu-anh Love

Introduction

Expressing gratitude is one of the most powerful ways to change your life from negative to positive and raise your vibrations from dark to light. From my own personal journey to a more happy, healthy and balanced lifestyle—besides talking to God, the Angels and to my higher self—writing in my gratitude journal daily has been the best form of therapy for me to cleanse my soul, brighten my days, and heal my heart of inner child wounds that have held me back from my truest potential. In addition to that, it is also the best way to manifest your dreams and desires into reality, especially during the New and the Full Moon periods.

No matter where I am traveling to at the moment, my gratitude journal is always with me. My morning coffee ritual includes being in solitude to pray, reflect, and go deep within my soul. And writing down the things that I am grateful for in my life helps make my day more productive, positive, and uplifting.

I designed this journal for myself, my clients, my students, and my mentees, and for all those who would like to embark on my Goddess Awakened journey. Let us begin by giving and sharing thanks each and every day to help make the world we live in a better place.

Happy journaling!

With much gratitude,
tu-anh Love

P.S. Just a little Goddess tip as you embark on this Awakened journey, try not to skip any days for a whole Moon cycle (29 days) if you really want to experience transformation.

Today I am grateful for . . .

Today I am grateful for . . .

Today I am grateful for . . .

Today I am grateful for . . .

Uplift your thoughts. Uplift your life.

Today I am grateful for . . .

Today I am grateful for . . .

Today I am grateful for . . .

Today I am grateful for . . .

Today I am grateful for . . .

Happiness is defined by you and you only.

Today I am grateful for . . .

Today I am grateful for . . .

Today I am grateful for . . .

Today I am grateful for . . .

Today I am grateful for . . .

Expressing gratitude daily will help us attract more abundance into our lives. What areas of your life could use more abundance?

Today I am grateful for . . .

Today I am grateful for . . .

Today I am grateful for . . .

Today I am grateful for . . .

Today I am grateful for . . .

The more we appreciate what we have, the more good things and blessings will come our way.

Today I am grateful for . . .

Today I am grateful for . . .

Today I am grateful for . . .

Today I am grateful for . . .

Today I am grateful for . . .

Anything is possible as long as you believe it is.

Today I am grateful for . . .

Today I am grateful for . . .

Today I am grateful for . . .

Today I am grateful for . . .

Today I am grateful for . . .

Giving gratitude each day is simple. It begins with the little things in our life and around us. Look around you, what do you see? What are you grateful for?

Today I am grateful for . . .

Today I am grateful for . . .

Today I am grateful for . . .

Today I am grateful for . . .

Today I am grateful for . . .

Begin each day with loving yourself a little more than yesterday.

Today I am grateful for...

Today I am grateful for . . .

Today I am grateful for . . .

Today I am grateful for . . .

Today I am grateful for . . .

Be ready, be open, pay attention. Listen to the sounds of nature. It can be your best therapist.

Today I am grateful for . . .

Today I am grateful for . . .

Today I am grateful for . . .

Today I am grateful for . . .

Today I am grateful for . . .

You don't have to answer to those who always want something from you. You only need to answer to your higher self.

Today I am grateful for . . .

Today I am grateful for . . .

Today I am grateful for . . .

Today I am grateful for . . .

Today I am grateful for . . .

Say yes when everyone else says no.

Today I am grateful for . . .

Today I am grateful for . . .

Today I am grateful for . . .

Today I am grateful for . . .

Today I am grateful for . . .

The way to happiness is not just about expressing gratitude, but also to forgive those who have hurt us and forget why they hurt us.

Today I am grateful for . . .

Today I am grateful for . . .

Today I am grateful for . . .

Today I am grateful for . . .

Today I am grateful for . . .

You only have one life to live. Make it the most magical and amazing ever!

Today I am grateful for ...

Today I am grateful for . . .

Today I am grateful for . . .

Today I am grateful for . . .

Today I am grateful for . . .

Love and appreciate all the good in your life at the moment because it may not be there tomorrow.

Today I am grateful for . . .

Today I am grateful for . . .

Today I am grateful for . . .

Today I am grateful for . . .

Today I am grateful for . . .

Don't ever, ever give up on yourself.

Today I am grateful for . . .

Today I am grateful for . . .

Today I am grateful for . . .

Today I am grateful for . . .

Today I am grateful for . . .

Surround yourself with those who are already living the life you love.

Today I am grateful for . . .

Today I am grateful for . . .

Today I am grateful for . . .

Today I am grateful for . . .

Today I am grateful for . . .

Today is the day that your life will change. Believe it.

Today I am grateful for . . .

Today I am grateful for . . .

Today I am grateful for . . .

Today I am grateful for . . .

Today I am grateful for . . .

To have more and attract more, you must become more.

Today I am grateful for . . .

Today I am grateful for . . .

Today I am grateful for . . .

Today I am grateful for . . .

Today I am grateful for . . .

Sometimes challenges and hardships come to us to teach us lessons and take us to the next chapter of our life. I am grateful for all the challenges that I have faced because they helped groom me to be the powerful and awakened Goddess that I am today.

Today I am grateful for . . .

Today I am grateful for . . .

Today I am grateful for . . .

Today I am grateful for . . .

Today I am grateful for . . .

Close your eyes,
listen to your heart.
It never lies.

Today I am grateful for . . .

Today I am grateful for . . .

Today I am grateful for...

Today I am grateful for . . .

Today I am grateful for . . .

Dreams do come true as long as we believe in them. I am grateful for living the life of my dreams.

Today I am grateful for . . .

Today I am grateful for . . .

Today I am grateful for . . .

Today I am grateful for . . .

Today I am grateful for . . .

Live each day as if it is the last day of your life.

Today I am grateful for . . .

Today I am grateful for . . .

Today I am grateful for . . .

Today I am grateful for . . .

Today I am grateful for . . .

Today I am grateful for . . .

Look in the mirror, tell yourself three times: I am grateful for you, my beautiful Goddess.

Today I am grateful for . . .

tu-anh Love

International fashion and life-style designer, beauty influencer, Divine teacher of the Awakened Feminine, trusted advisor and personal style goddess to the Awakened Masculine, model, spiritual dancer, humanitarian, and lover of life.

Born in Nha Trang, Vietnam, and currently residing between Washington D.C. and the Pacific Coast of Mexico, tu-anh was raised to value the arts, culture, tradition, and humanities. She was especially influenced by her mother's ability to act, speak, and hustle with style and grace, never sacrificing her femininity and sensuality.

Today, tu-anh's mission is to help modern-day women from all around the world awaken the inner Goddess within and embrace their beauty, style, and grace as blessed strengths—helping to fill the world with unconditional love, Divine light, harmonious balance, and inner peace.

"Every woman has an inner goddess, and everyone wants to be with her"

-tu-anh Love

Have questions or gratitude success stories to share?
Email tuanhlovegoddess@gmail.com

Made in the USA
Columbia, SC
08 April 2023

f47b11b1-af69-454d-b0f3-10bb7a99f60dR01